Supporting Dyslexic Learners in the Second
Moira Thomson, MBE

DYSLEXIA: DRAMA
(Performing Arts; Theatre Studies)

First published in Great Britain by Dyslexia Scotland in 2007

Second edition for schools in England published in 2017 by CPD Bytes Ltd

ISBN 978-1-912146-37-6

This booklet is 2.2 in the series
Supporting Dyslexic Learners in the Secondary Curriculum (England)

Supporting Dyslexic Learners in the Secondary Curriculum   Moira Thomson, MBE
Complete set comprises 25 booklets

1.0   Dyslexia: Secondary Teachers' Guides

1.1   Identification and Assessment of Dyslexia at Secondary School
1.2   Dyslexia: Underpinning Skills for the Secondary Curriculum
1.3   Dyslexia: Reasonable Adjustments to Classroom Management
1.4   Dyslexia: Role of the Secondary School SENCo (Dyslexia Specialist Teacher)
1.5   Partnerships with Parents of Secondary School Students with Dyslexia
1.6   Dyslexia: ICT Support in the Secondary Curriculum
1.7   Dyslexia: Examinations (Reasonable Adjustments & Access Arrangements)
1.8   Dyslexia: Information for Guidance, Pastoral & Behaviour Support Teachers (2013)
1.9   Dyslexia: Learning Styles and Study Skills for the Secondary Curriculum NEW
1.10   Dyslexia: Role of the Teaching Assistant NEW
1.11   Dyslexia: Co-occurring & Overlapping Issues (Specific Learning Difficulties) NEW

2.0   Dyslexia: Subject Teachers' Guides

2.1   Dyslexia: Art & Design Subjects
2.2   Dyslexia: Drama (Performing Arts; Theatre Studies)
2.3   Dyslexia: English (Communication)
2.4   Dyslexia: Home Economics (Child Development; Food & Nutrition)
2.5   Dyslexia: ICT Subjects (Business Subjects; Computer Science)
2.6   Dyslexia: Mathematics (Statistics)
2.7   Dyslexia: Modern Foreign Languages
2.8   Dyslexia: Music
2.9   Dyslexia: Physical Education (Sports; Games; Dance)
2.10   Dyslexia: Science Subjects (Biology; Chemistry; General Science; Physics)
2.11   Dyslexia: Social Subjects (Economics; Geography; History; Citizenship Studies; Philosophy; Religious Studies)
2.12   Dyslexia: The Classics (Classical Greek; Latin; Classical Civilisations) (2013)
2.13   Dyslexia: Media Studies NEW
2.14   Dyslexia: Social Sciences (Anthropology; Archaeology; Humanities; Psychology; Sociology) NEW

Foreword by Dr Gavin Reid, formerly senior lecturer in the Department of Educational Studies, Moray House School of Education, University of Edinburgh. An experienced teacher, educational psychologist, university lecturer, researcher and author, he has made over 1000 conference and seminar presentations in more than 40 countries and has authored, co-authored and edited many books for teachers and parents.

ACKNOWLEDGEMENTS

Moira Thomson would like to thank the following for making possible the original publication of this important series of booklets:

+ Dyslexia Scotland for supporting the publication and distribution of the original editions of these booklets

+ The Royal Bank of Scotland for an education grant that funded Dyslexia Scotland's support

+ Dr Gavin Reid for his encouragement over the years – and for writing the Foreword to these booklets

+ Dr Jennie Guise of DysGuise Ltd for her support and professional advice

+ The committee of Dyslexia Scotland South East for their support

+ Alasdair Andrew for all his hard work and unfailing confidence

+ Colleagues Maggie MacLardie and Janet Hodgson for helpful comments

+ Cameron Halfpenny for proof reading and editing these booklets

+ Current and former students, whose achievements make it all worthwhile

Moira Thomson MBE

2017

FOREWORD by Dr Gavin Reid

The Dyslexia booklets written by Moira Thomson have been widely circulated and highly appreciated by teachers throughout Scotland and beyond. I know they have also been used by teachers in a number of countries and this is testimony to the skills of Moira in putting together these booklets in the different subject areas of the secondary school curriculum.

It is therefore an additional privilege for me to be approached again by Moira to update this Foreword to the compendium of books developed by Moira in association with Dyslexia Scotland.

These updated guides are for all teachers - they contain information that will be directly relevant and directly impact on the practice of every teacher in every secondary school in the country. It is heartening to note that the guides again provide a very positive message to readers. The term Dyslexia is not exclusive to the challenges experienced by learners with dyslexia, but there is now a major thrust towards focussing on the strengths and particularly what they **can** do - and not what they 'can't do'. It is important to obtain a learning profile which can be shared with the student.

Moira encapsulates these points in these updated booklets. The focus is on supporting learners and helping them overcome the barriers to learning. At the same time it is important that learners with dyslexia, particularly in the secondary school develop responsibility for their own learning. The acquisition of self-sufficiency in learning and self-knowledge is an important aspect of acquiring efficient learning skills for students with dyslexia. It is this that will stand them in good stead as they approach important examinations and the transition to tertiary education and the workplace. For that reason these guides are extremely important and need to be available to all teachers. Moira ought to be congratulated in endeavouring to achieve this.

The breadth of coverage in these guides is colossal. Moira Thomson has met this immense task with professionalism and clarity of expression and the comprehensiveness of the guides in covering the breadth of the curriculum is commendable.

As well as including all secondary school subjects the guides also provide information on the crucial aspects of supporting students preparing for examinations, the use of information and communication technology, information for parents, details of the assessment process and the skills that underpin learning. It is important to consider the view that learners with dyslexia are first and foremost 'learners' and therefore it is important that their learning skills are developed fully. It is too easy to place the emphasis on developing literacy skills at the expense of other important aspects of learning. The guides will reinforce this crucial point that the learning skills of all students with dyslexia can be developed to a high level.

The guides do more than provide information on dyslexia; they are a staff development resource and one that can enlighten and educate all teachers in secondary schools. I feel certain they will continue to be warmly appreciated. The guides have already been widely appreciated by teachers and school management as well as parents and other professionals, but the real winners have been and will continue to be the **students** with dyslexia. It is they who will ultimately benefit and the guides will help them fulfil their potential and make learning a positive and successful school experience.

Dr Gavin Reid
April 2016

WHAT IS DYSLEXIA?

Dyslexia is widely recognised as a specific difficulty in learning to read.

Research shows that dyslexia may affect more than the ability to read, write and spell – and there is a growing body of research on these 'co-occurring' factors.

The Rose Report[1] identifies dyslexia as *'a developmental difficulty of language learning and cognition that primarily affects the skills involved in accurate and fluent word reading and spelling, characterised by difficulties in phonological awareness, verbal memory and verbal processing speed.'*

Dyslexia is a learning difficulty that primarily affects the skills involved in accurate and fluent word reading and spelling.

Characteristic features of dyslexia are difficulties in phonological awareness, verbal memory and verbal processing speed.

Dyslexia occurs across the range of intellectual abilities.

It is best thought of as a continuum, not a distinct category, and there are no clear cut-off points.

Co-occurring difficulties may be seen in aspects of language, motor co-ordination, mental calculation, concentration and personal organisation, but these are not, <u>by themselves,</u> markers of dyslexia.

A good indication of the severity and persistence of dyslexic difficulties can be gained by examining how the individual responds or has responded to well-founded intervention.

Rose Report page 10

Dyslexia exists in all cultures and across the range of abilities and socio-economic backgrounds. It is a hereditary, life-long, neuro-developmental condition. Unidentified, dyslexia is likely to result in low self-esteem, high stress, atypical behaviour, and low achievement.[2]

Estimates of the prevalence of dyslexia vary according to the definition adopted but research suggests that dyslexia may significantly affect the literacy attainment of between 4% and 10% of children.

---

[1] Rose, J (2009) *Identifying and Teaching Children and Young People with Dyslexia and Literacy Difficulties* DCFS Publications - independent report to the Secretary of State for Children, Schools & Families June 2009 http://webarchive.nationalarchives.gov.uk/20130401151715/http://www.education.gov.uk/publications/eOr deringDownload/00659-2009DOM-EN.pdf

[2] From Scottish Government working definition of dyslexia http://www.gov.scot/Topics/Education/Schools/welfare/ASL/dyslexia

TEACHERS' RESPONSIBILITIES RE LEARNERS WITH DYSLEXIA

References: Part 6 of the Equality Act 2010; Part 3 of the Children and Families Act 2014

All children/young people are entitled to an education appropriate to their needs that promotes high standards and the fulfilment of potential - to enable them to:

- achieve their best
- become confident individuals living fulfilling lives
- make a successful transition into adulthood, whether into employment, further or higher education or training

SEND Code of Practice 0-25[3]

All schools have duties towards individual young people to identify and address any Special Educational Needs/Disability (SEND). Dyslexia that has a substantial, long-term, adverse impact on day-to-day learning may be identified as both SEN and a disability.

Teachers' responsibilities for meeting the needs of dyslexic learners are the same as those for all students, and should include approaches that avoid unnecessary dependence on written text.

Teachers have a responsibility to provide a suitably differentiated subject curriculum, accessible to all learners, that provides each with the opportunity to develop and apply individual strengths – and to ensure that learners with SEND get the support they need to access this. Rose[4] suggests that all teachers should have 'core knowledge' of dyslexia characteristics – to help them to make adjustments to their practice that will prevent discrimination and substantial disadvantage.

Dyslexia may be difficult for some teachers to identify in a subject context – some think that dyslexia has little or no impact in their subject – others believe that dyslexia will have been resolved at primary school. The impact of unsupported dyslexia on learning in secondary subject classrooms may be profound, and result in a mismatch between a student's apparent subject ability and the quality (and quantity) of written work.

While subject teachers are not expected to diagnose dyslexia without specialist input, they should be aware of its core characteristics and likely manifestations in the classroom so they may refer students to the SENCo (or specialist teacher) for assessment. Many schools have checklists and questionnaires in place to help teachers identify possible SEN and subject teachers should use these and follow established procedures when they suspect that dyslexia might be present.[5]

---

[3] SEND Code of Practice 0-25
https://www.gov.uk/government/uploads/system/uploads/attachment_data/file/398815/SEND_Code_of_Practice_January_2015.pdf
[4] Rose Report (2009) page 17
[5] A version of a Dyslexia Indicators Checklist for secondary age students is provided at the end of this booklet

SUBJECT TEACHERS' GRADUATED APPROACH TO DYSLEXIA SUPPORT SHOULD INCLUDE:

- Recognition of and sensitivity to the range and diversity of the learning preferences and styles of all learners

- Awareness of the learning differences related to dyslexia that may cause difficulties within the subject curriculum

    o Acknowledgement of the very severe difficulties some dyslexic learners experience due to failure to master early stages of literacy and numeracy

    o Understanding that dyslexia is developmental in nature and that some students who coped with the early stages of literacy acquisition may begin to experience difficulties with higher order skills and processing issues in the secondary curriculum

- Selection or design of appropriate teaching and learning programmes that match the range of all abilities, within the curricular framework of the school

- Commitment to the need to reduce barriers to learning linked to the delivery of the curriculum as well as those due to the impact of dyslexia

- Acceptance that some learners with dyslexia may require additional support within the context of a subject and to consult with parents, colleagues and specialists (and the young person) to determine how best to provide this

- Willingness to ask for advice and support from the SENCo and/or specialist teacher if a dyslexic learner does not make the expected progress towards achieving outcomes identified in the SEN Support Plan

- Understanding that, while dyslexia is not linked to ability, able dyslexic learners may persistently underachieve

- Knowledge that many dyslexic learners use strategies such as misbehaviour or illness for coping with difficulties they do not necessarily understand themselves

- Taking account of the difficulties experienced by dyslexic learners when reviewing progress so that subject knowledge and ability are assessed fairly by making reasonable adjustments to arrangements for assessments (Access Arrangements) that reflect the additional support usually provided in the classroom

Dyslexic learners constantly meet barriers to learning across the curriculum and may become discouraged very quickly due to lack of initial success in subject classes. This may result in subject teachers assuming that they are inattentive or lazy, when they are actually working much harder than their classmates, but with little apparent effect.

DRAMA CLASSROOMS/STUDIOS

It is important that secondary teachers consider dyslexia in the context of their own subject. In any subject class there will be a need to make provision to meet a wide variety of strengths and learning needs, not all linked to dyslexia, but adjustments to teaching and learning approaches that are appropriate for dyslexic learners can be effective for all.

A dyslexic student may fully understand the teacher's spoken introduction to a topic but be unable to follow written instructions for class activities. For many learners with dyslexia the experience of success may be rare. They may:
- be very disorganised and confuse written and verbal instructions
- appear to avoid set work (because of confusion about what is required)
- fear new situations
- approach new tasks with an expectation of failure
- lack stamina and be vulnerable to fatigue
- lack self-confidence and have a poor self-image

Drama and Theatre Studies provide many dyslexic learners with an opportunity to excel, since they may think in pictures, sounds or actions rather than words – recent neurological research shows an association between visual talents and verbal difficulties. Dyslexic differences that make learning to read, write and spell difficult may be linked to high ability where imagination and visual perception are important and individual interpretation is required.

Drama now extends beyond theatre into television, film, radio and computer-based media though direct engagement with professional theatre is an essential part of the drama curriculum, complementing and enriching teaching and learning at all stages of education. Through engagement in drama, students apply their imaginations and draw upon their own personal experiences to shape, express and share their ideas, feelings and responses, making use of language, space, symbol, allegory and metaphor.

Dyslexic students may experience some problems when e.g. researching the historical or cultural background of a play to contribute to set/costume design – but excel when experimenting with sound or lighting to set or transform a mood, contributing to an improvisation or devising an original piece of work.

Although performance - ranging from imaginative role-play in the classroom to scripted performances in a drama studio – is often a strength of those with dyslexia, their literacy, memory, processing, visual and motor skills issues may have an adverse impact on attainment in some aspects of this subject.

Dyslexic people often become very successful in Drama, Theatre and Performance Arts:

- Acting
- Mime
- Directing
- Film/TV production
- Script writing

- Set/lighting design
- Animation
- Stage management
- Costume design
- Sound engineering

Significant strengths of dyslexic students of Drama and Theatre Studies may include:

- Strongly developed spatial awareness – with multi-dimensional thinking and perception and an acute awareness of the environment
- A multi-sensory learning style that encompasses all aspects of performance
- Keen observation skills and fast reaction times
- Excellent oral skills – especially mimicry and timing and an intrinsic ability to relate movement to speech
- Good reasoning and enquiry skills - an ability to draw inferences and make deductions by asking relevant questions and testing conclusions
- Excellent kinaesthetic memory - linking script lines to stage movement
- Excellence in computer graphics and animation – computer use may enhance the creative potential of visual thinkers/directors/set designers
- Empathic, highly intuitive and perceptive
- Creative with a vivid imagination - often a quirky and original sense of humour able to generate and extend ideas and look for alternative endings

BARRIERS TO LEARNING

The underpinning literacy difficulties of many dyslexic students that impact learning in all areas of the curriculum may be less of an issue in the Drama studio where alternative forms of communication are studied and celebrated.

Students with dyslexia often experience processing issues and lack fluency and automaticity when reading/writing – despite excellent oral skills - so they may take more time than others to think, question, deduce or form opinions before responding to a visual or auditory stimulus. Those who also experience specific difficulties in Maths may be further disadvantaged when calculation, measurement and direction are required in practical activities. Self-esteem and confidence issues and the cumulative effect of fatigue may have a powerful impact on dyslexic students' ability to cope with some of the performance demands of the Drama/Theatre Arts curriculum.

It is not expected that all students with dyslexia will experience all of the difficulties identified below – so teachers may wish to ask individuals to identify issues they experience in Drama activities so that reasonable adjustments to meet SEN can be made and any additional required support planned and provided. A downloadable version of the list below is provided at the end of this booklet

BARRIERS TO LEARNING - LITERACY ISSUES

Reading: students with dyslexia may

- be unable to read scripts, texts for improvisation etc. accurately in good time
- give up easily when faced with long texts and small print
- have difficulty locating, reading and assimilating information in text sources or on a board
- continually lose the place or read the wrong lines or mispronounce words when script reading and be unable to pick up from where they left off
- experience visual disorientation when reading printed material so they are unable to concentrate for any length of time
- be unable to proof read or identify errors in their own work

Writing: students with dyslexia may

- be unable to write quickly and legibly when developing material
- struggle to copy, annotate scripts or take dictated notes
- lack fluency when writing due to word-finding, spelling and sequencing issues
- lose the thread when they are writing resulting in messy and poorly sequenced work
- be unable to write in the required format e.g. cannot add stage directions to scripted speech
- produce only brief written pieces that do not reflect the full extent of their subject knowledge and understanding

BARRIERS TO LEARNING - COMMUNICATION ISSUES

Listening/watching: students with dyslexia may

- be unable to respond appropriately in improvisation/role play due to the need to process language before being able to process content
- lose track of what is spoken by whom in a studio or on screen
- be unable to concentrate on listening/watching due to visual distractions and background noise
- appear not to listen in discussion/brainstorming groups

Talking: students with dyslexia may

- lose track of what they are saying – often repeating themselves or 'drying up' completely
- struggle to use correct vocabulary – they may feel humiliated when they mispronounce words or use the 'wrong' word
- have difficulty with waiting for cues – interrupting others or speaking out of turn because they know they will forget their own lines if they wait
- not contribute to discussions as they find that their comment is no longer relevant

BARRIERS TO LEARNING - STUDY SKILLS ISSUES

Processing: students with dyslexia may

- take longer than others to respond to direction/instructions
- have difficulty planning, sequencing and keeping to a story line when improvising/ developing coherent scripts
- misinterpret written instructions – leading to e.g. carrying out the wrong task
- tire more quickly than others when reading/writing so that the quality of work deteriorates over the course of a lesson
- sacrifice originality and creativity to complete an activity in the time allowed

Working memory: students with dyslexia may

- struggle with working memory, so be unable to remember lines and direction/ instructions from one moment to the next
- forget what character they are trying to represent
- have difficulty remembering to carry props etc. on to the stage
- misunderstand complex sequences of instructions
- struggle to carry out a sequence of actions in the right order

BARRIERS TO LEARNING - PRACTICAL ACTIVITIES ISSUES

Organisational: some students with dyslexia may

- have difficulty organising work space – misplace props and equipment
- have difficulty finding/keeping the place in a script, locating director's notes in a workbook or finding files on a computer
- be unable to cope with stage directions – e.g. left/right, forward/back etc. – so may be unable to move as directed or direct others effectively
- have difficulty following a sequence of instructions in the right order, with an adverse impact on stage movement and directing skills
- sacrifice originality and creativity to complete an activity in the time allowed

Motor Skills: some students with dyslexia may

- be clumsy, bump into things or knock them over on stage or in a studio space
- may be unable to co-ordinate movements or plan sequential movements when using props/equipment
- experience problems with automaticity of fine and gross motor skills resulting in clumsiness when using e.g. cameras or a lighting desk
- experience weaknesses and increasing fatigue with some aspects of stage movement

REASONABLE ADJUSTMENTS

Teachers should identify the required course outcomes for all students and use differentiated resources/tasks when implementing graduated SEN support strategies to remove barriers to learning for dyslexic students in Drama activities.

LITERACY ~~issues~~

Reading:

- Always issue set scripts well in advance so that dyslexic students can prepare for reading aloud
- Issue large print scripts to help dyslexic students to find the place more easily
- Highlight and use colour codes for character names/lines in scripts so students can find their own parts quickly
- Reduce distortions by allowing use of coloured paper and tinted overlays
- Vary classroom/studio lighting to minimise glare and visual stress

Writing:

- Encourage the use of ICT for script production and other writing activities e.g. scenery and set design notes
- Encourage the use of bullet points, mind maps and visual representation for developing story lines
- Model/provide 'skeleton' versions of the required format of written responses
- Provide visual, audio or electronic versions of notes and instructions
- Provide an electronic word list to help with spelling for internet searches

COMMUNICATION

Listening/watching:

- Ensure that key subject information is read aloud only by a competent reader
- Add visual or kinaesthetic support to enable dyslexic students to recognise spoken cues – e.g. adding a gesture or facial expression
- Provide transcripts of audio/video source material so the dyslexic student can identify e.g. spoken input by different characters
- Create visual, audio or electronic versions of notes and stage directions so dyslexic performers can focus on listening/watching instead of trying to take notes
- Provide a concentration focus for listening – doodling or colouring a visual representation related to the topic

Talking:

- Initially, allow some 'thinking time' for dyslexic students to give oral responses
- Teach the use of prompt cards and slide presentations for sequencing and illustrating oral presentations – and learning lines
- Arrange for turn-taking signals when brainstorming to enable students with dyslexia to contribute ideas as they occur to ensure that originality and creativity is not lost

- Be aware that short-term memory problems contribute to difficulties with learning lines and remembering cues
- Be aware that while some dyslexic learners will excel at 'brainstorming' others may be completely unable to participate

STUDY SKILLS
Processing:

- Design simple annotations on scripts - use pictures and symbols as well as words - to show stage or technical directions – and use these for all similar activities
- Use large-print prompt cards for instructions, stage lighting cues etc.
- Allow extra time for dyslexic learners to practice skills and techniques and learn lines
- Use prompts and arrows to indicate directions – ensure that dyslexic students understand the difference in perspective between, e.g. right and stage right
- Keep improvisation and design activities as open-ended as possible – allow a range of styles or outcomes
- Encourage students to try different approaches to/interpretations of activities
- Build-in diversions/rest periods to lesson plans to minimise fatigue

Working memory:

- Arrange extra time and rehearsals for dyslexic students to learn lines
- Repeat a series of instructions one at a time and relate these to gestures or stage moves where possible
- Number the steps or devise flow charts for designing e.g. sound or lighting scripts – or provide checklists starting with 'switch on'
- Develop a mantra for remembering props – e.g. use 'rap' or action poems to be recited before going onstage
- Permit the use of memory aids for routine activities – e.g. a rubber band on the wrist to indicate stage left
- Suggest reminders for practical activities – e.g. different coloured marks on the stage to show positions, sticky notes on the sound script to indicate the sound effects

PRACTICAL SKILLS
Organisation:

- Repeat a series of instructions one at a time and relate these to visual demonstrations of actions or equipment use where possible
- Number the steps or devise flow charts to help with sequencing and developing automaticity of stage movement
- Design simple annotations on story-boards and scripts to show technical directions – and use these for all similar activities
- Provide blank copies of rehearsal schedules, diagrams, charts etc. for completion, clearly indicating where information should go

Motor Skills:

- Arrange additional hands-on time for dyslexic students to practice skills and techniques so they may become proficient in the use of equipment
- Demonstrate and model techniques e.g. to indicate character age
- Break down performance movements into a series of very small steps and model these
- Issue costumes and props as early as possible to help students move appropriately and keep in character
- Help learners to develop rhythm in practical activities e.g. use music, beating time, tapping feet etc. - develop a dance routine for e.g. setting up a camera

It is important that teachers make a note of the differentiation and adjustments they make in the classroom and for course-related activities so that they can verify an individual's usual way of working when applying for access arrangements for written exams.

REASONABLE ADJUSTMENTS/ACCESS ARRANGEMENTS FOR ASSESSMENTS

The Joint Council for Qualifications (JCQ)[6] - and other awarding bodies who have the responsibility of making reasonable adjustments for a candidate defined as disabled within the meaning of the Equality Act 2010 who would be at a substantial disadvantage in comparison to someone who is not disabled – are required to take reasonable steps to overcome that disadvantage. They must offer a range of reasonable adjustments (Access) to arrangements for dyslexic candidates taking examinations.

Access arrangements are agreed before an assessment to meet the specific needs of individual candidates without affecting the integrity of the assessment. They allow candidates with dyslexia to:
- access the assessment (e.g. a printed exam paper or design brief)
- show what they know and can do without changing the demands of the assessment

These adjustments are designed to reflect the support provided for dyslexic candidates in the subject curriculum and to address any specific difficulties/disadvantage caused by the style of an assessment/examination and its impact on the opportunities for them to demonstrate actual attainment – without compromising the integrity of the assessment.

Examination papers are not changed – or made easier - in any way and marking criteria remain the same as for all examination candidates.

The range of access arrangements/reasonable adjustments available for dyslexic candidates in written exams includes:
- Linguistic support (reader, computer screen reader, reading aloud, use of reading pen, digital examination papers, scribe, transcription with correction)
- Extra time allowances (25%; up to/over 50%)
- ICT - use of word processors with spellcheckers, specialised software and other technological aids
- Coloured/enlarged paper (e.g. A3 unmodified enlarged papers)

A reasonable adjustment may be unique to an individual and is not included in the list of available access arrangements - but it may be arranged directly with the JCQ. However, some adjustments are not possible for some qualifications – e.g. a human reader is not permitted for an assessment that tests reading.

If assessment instructions are given orally, dyslexic candidates may need to have these repeated, often more than once – or be provided with a printed version of these. Some dyslexic candidates may ask for specific seating/work station arrangements in exams to take account of the impact of ambient lighting, noise levels etc.

---

[6] Every September, the JCQ publishes regulations for access arrangements for examinations. These can be downloaded from http://www.jcq.org.uk/exams-office/access-arrangements-and-special-consideration

Exam questions and marking standards remain the same for all candidates – access changes are to the format of an exam only, where these place a dyslexic candidate at a substantial disadvantage – e.g. by removing the support usually provided for subject course work.

In schools, the SENCo - supported by subject teaching staff and the senior leadership team – leads the access arrangements process to determine and implement appropriate access arrangements for dyslexic students. **Approved access arrangements must be put in place for internal school tests, mock examinations and formal examinations.**

Drama teachers should note that dyslexic students may not require access arrangements for the performance of their examination productions in a public showcase - though these may be required at the preparation stage of devising and scripting performance materials. Similarly, those dyslexic students who choose the option to study technical aspects of theatre such as lighting, sound and design may need reasonable adjustments for the design planning stage for internal assessments that involve making notes or reading to prepare for an activity. If practical assessment instructions are given orally, dyslexic students may need to have these repeated, possibly several times

Access arrangements are most likely to be needed by students with dyslexia for time-limited written exams of knowledge and understanding of dramatic theory and different dramatic techniques and forms - when literacy weaknesses may have a substantial adverse impact.

Evidence of a candidate's usual way of working
The SENCo will have evidence of a formal assessment of a candidate's dyslexia and of the need for access arrangements. However, subject teachers must describe the reasonable adjustments (or differentiation) they usually provide in the classroom - whether for all students or individually for a candidate with dyslexia. This will explain a student's usual way of working and will be entered on access arrangements application to JCQ.[7]

If a Drama teacher always arranges for live or recorded readings of plays for a whole class, this is evidence that a dyslexic student is accustomed to a human reader in the subject. If a student with dyslexia dictates - e.g. scripted dialogue or stage directions - to another pupil or audio-recorder, this is evidence of the student's usual way of producing written work.

While dyslexic students may not require significant adjustments in the performance aspects of Drama – they may need more time than their classmates to complete written aspects of a course. If a student habitually fails to meet deadlines for written assignments, often has to complete written exercises at home or after class and/or has incomplete pieces of work in a design folio, this may be evidence of the need for extra time for written work. Subject teachers' arrangements of time for a student to complete essential course work are evidence that extra time is the usual way of working.

---

[7] JCQ Form 8 section A – completed by SENCo or specialist assessor

ROLE MODELS FOR DYSLEXIC LEARNERS

When at school, the impact of dyslexic difficulties often outweighs natural abilities in a subject area resulting in underachievement and lack of confidence and self-esteem. Teachers of successful dyslexic individuals often express surprise – or astonishment – at their achievements after they have left formal schooling behind.

Perhaps awareness of some people who have already succeeded may be the best guide to promote understanding of how to create success where there is so often failure. The abilities of many dyslexics seem to be particularly clear in the entertainment industry where achievement is measured by success, which is often more highly valued in society than traditional academic skills and paper credentials.

The high numbers of dyslexic learners in the acting profession may suggest that dyslexia is not a 'deficit' but a strength. After all, many actors view dyslexia as a source of their creativity. The following personal comments and histories may offer insight into dyslexia.

Former *EastEnders* actress **Carol Harrison** recognised that: *"...having dyslexia has made me a better actor because instead of just saying the words, you have to feel them very, very deeply, take them inside of yourself, process them and bring them out again."* While **Kara Tointon** revealed that difficulties, such as sight reading, can be a major barrier to audition success and her struggle to learn lines led her to adopt successful multi-sensory learning.

Actor and comedian **Eddie Izzard** believes that *"dyslexia tends to make you go off in a weird direction"* and helps him to think outside the box.

Fred Newman suggests that precisely because of poor working memory his *"dyslexia forces [him] to continually live in the moment, to be more creative."*

Film director **Guy Ritchie** is very dyslexic and his abilities were completely masked by this at school. Although he couldn't write he had an awful lot to say. But all anyone ever did was teach him remedial Maths and remedial English.

Orlando Bloom, one of the busiest and most sought after actors in the industry, struggled in many subjects at school because of his dyslexia. But he did well in the arts and enjoyed pottery, photography and sculpture as well as performing in school plays – eventually going on to drama college and a successful career.

Tom Cruise was made fun of by other kids because of his dyslexia – an experience that made him tough inside and able to quietly accept abuse and ridicule and succeed in a very public career. He found learning demanded a terrific effort as *"pages turned to meaningless blocks of weird scribbles"* before his eyes.

Movies helped **Steven Spielberg** cope with his dyslexia. As a child, Spielberg said he learned to read two years later than his classmates, which made him subject to teasing and caused him to dread school.

Whoopi Goldberg: *"What you can never change is the effect that the words 'dumb' and 'stupid' have on young people. I found out I was dyslexic when I was a grown woman. When I was a kid they didn't call it dyslexia. They called it... you know, you were slow, or you were retarded, or whatever."*

Successful actress **Keira Knightley,** as a dyslexic schoolgirl, struggled with lessons and was considered stupid by classmates, but teachers now remember her as one of the top pupils in her year – paying little heed to the hours of extra tutoring she required to succeed at school. *"I certainly wasn't one of the popular people. When I was little, kids called me stupid because I couldn't read."*

Danny Glover: *"Kids made fun of me because I was dyslexic. Even as an actor, it took me a long time to realize why words and letters got jumbled in my mind and came out differently."*

Sir Anthony Hopkins had an *"awful"* childhood because he was so hopeless at school. He was a moody, lonely, only child whose main pleasure was playing the piano and whose father worried about him not being like other boys. *"I feel more responsive to other people because I'm not so insecure. I just feel reassured that I wasn't the moron I thought I was."*

Salma Hayek, considered by many to be the most successful Latin actor in Hollywood, having appeared in more than thirty films and secured a nomination for an Oscar: *"...one day I could not say the lines right. I'm dyslexic and I was tired."*

The late **Robin Williams** was known for his wild improvisation skills and impersonations. He was a talented mimic and could jump in and out of characters at an extremely fast pace. His remarkable creativity and intense impulsive humour was linked to his dyslexia – though he may have had co-occurring ADHD.

Jay Leno, TV talk show host, is dyslexic and got mainly Cs and Ds in school. *"One thing about many dyslexic people — they're good at setting everything else aside to pursue one goal - I'm an example of success through persistence."*

Charley Boorman is an actor, adventurer and a writer. He is also dyslexic. *"At the time when I was going to school in Ireland people didn't really have a clue about what it was, so I had to spend a lot of my time trying to explain to teachers what dyslexia meant."* Frustrated in class, he played the clown. *"I found I was being pushed to one side and I was being ear-marked as being thick, which is a very damaging thing to be told as a young kid."*

FURTHER READING

Eadon, H (2004) *Dyslexia and Drama* London, David Fulton Publishers
This book is designed to help teachers enable dyslexic students to get the most from drama inside and outside the classroom. It covers:

- a straightforward explanation of dyslexia
- tactics for removing problems experienced by students in drama lessons
- suggestions for setting homework
- ideas to boost students exam success
- insights into good and bad practice with case studies

Gray, R (2001) *Drama: the Experience of Learning* IN Peer, L & Reid, G (2001): *Dyslexia – Successful Inclusion in the Secondary School* London, David Fulton Publishers

Leveroy, D (2012) *Dyslexia and Sight Reading for Actors* IN *Music, Other Performing Arts and Dyslexia* Ed. Sally Daunt London, British Dyslexia Association

Leveroy, D (2013) *Locating dyslexic performance: text, identity and creativity* Research in *Drama Education* 18.4 (November 2013)

Leveroy, D (2015) *A Date with the Script - exploring the learning strategies of actors who are dyslexic* IN *Theatre, Dance and Performance Training* (November 2015)

MacKay, N (2005) *Removing Dyslexia as a Barrier to Achievement: The Dyslexia Friendly Schools Toolkit* 3rd Edition (2012) Wakefield, SEN Marketing

Rooke, M (2015) *Creative Successful Dyslexic* London, Jessica Kingsley Publishers
23 very well-known people from the arts, sport, and business worlds talk about how dyslexia affected their childhoods and how they were able to overcome the challenges and use the special strengths of dyslexia to achieve great success in adulthood.

Thomson, M (2007) *Supporting Students with Dyslexia at Secondary School – every class teacher's guide to removing barriers and raising attainment* London, Routledge Chs. 5 & 6

Thomson, M (2008) *Dyslexia and Inclusion at Secondary School* IN Reid et al (Ed.) 2008 *The SAGE Handbook of Dyslexia* London, Sage

West, TG (1997) *In the Mind's Eye: Visual Thinkers, Gifted People with Learning Difficulties, Computer Images and the Ironies of Creativity* Loughton, Prometheus

DYSLEXIA INDICATORS AT THE SECONDARY STAGE (PHOTOCOPIABLE)

Dyslexia is more than an isolated defect in reading or spelling. The problem may be perceptual, auditory receptive, memory-based or a processing deficit.

Subject teachers are not expected to be able to diagnose these difficulties as such, but some general indications are listed below. If several of these are observed frequently in the classroom, subject teachers should tick the relevant boxes to identify issues when referring a student for further investigation.

Student Name: _____ Class: _____ Date: _____

- ❑ Quality of written work does not adequately reflect the known ability of the student in the subject

- ❑ Good orally but very little written work is produced – many incomplete assignments

- ❑ Disappointing performance in timed tests and other assessments

- ❑ Poor presentation of work – e.g. illegibility, mixed upper and lower case, unequal spacing, copying errors, misaligned columns (especially in Maths)

- ❑ Poor organisational skills – the student is unable to organise self or work efficiently; carries either all books or wrong ones; frequently forgets to hand in work

- ❑ Sequencing poor – student appears to jump from one theme to another, apparently for no reason

- ❑ Inability to memorise (especially in Maths and Modern Languages) even after repeated practice

- ❑ Inability to hold numbers in short-term memory while performing calculations

- ❑ Symbol and shape confusion (especially in Maths)

- ❑ Complains of headaches when reading; sometimes sees patterns/distortions in printed text; says that words move around the page or that text is glaring at them

- ❑ Unable to carry out operations one day which were previously done adequately

- ❑ Unable to take in and carry out more than one instruction at a time

- ❑ Poor depth perception – e.g. clumsy and uncoordinated, bumps into things, difficulty judging distance, catching balls, etc.

- ❑ Poor self-image – lacking in confidence, fear of new situations – may erase large quantities of written work, which is acceptable to the teacher

- ❑ Tires quickly and work seems to be a disproportionate return for the effort involved in producing it

- ❑ Easily distracted – either hyperactive or daydreaming

- ❑ **Other – details below**

Teacher: _____ Subject: _____

Action requested:

- ❑ details of known SEND

- ❑ investigation of SEND and advice on graduated support

- ❑ dyslexia assessment

- ❑ profile of additional learning needs

- ❑ suggest reasonable adjustments to be made in class

- ❑ suggest SEN support strategies to meet needs in class

- ❑ advice re Access arrangements

DRAMA/THEATRE ARTS: BARRIERS TO LEARNING FOR STUDENTS WITH DYSLEXIA
(PHOTOCOPIABLE)

Not all students with dyslexia will experience all of the listed barriers to learning in Media Studies. It is suggested that students highlight those issues that they do experience and add any other barriers or problems they encounter in class to the list. Students should share this information with the Drama teacher – and use it to discuss the reasonable adjustments that might be made to minimise or remove these barriers and improve attainment.

BARRIERS TO LEARNING - LITERACY ISSUES
Reading:
- ❑ unable to read scripts, text sources for improvisation etc. accurately in good time
- ❑ give up easily when faced with long texts and small print
- ❑ difficulty locating, reading and assimilating information in text sources or on a board
- ❑ continually lose the place or read the wrong lines or mispronounce words when script reading and unable to pick up from the same place
- ❑ experience visual disorientation when reading printed material so unable to concentrate for any length of time
- ❑ unable to proof read or identify errors in written work

Additional reading issues:

Writing:
- ❑ unable to write quickly and legibly when developing material
- ❑ struggle to copy, annotate scripts or take dictated notes
- ❑ lack fluency when writing due to word-finding, spelling and sequencing issues
- ❑ lose the thread when writing resulting in messy and poorly sequenced work
- ❑ unable to write as required e.g. cannot add stage directions to scripted speech
- ❑ produce only brief written pieces that do not reflect the full extent of subject knowledge and understanding

Additional writing issues:

BARRIERS TO LEARNING - COMMUNICATION ISSUES
Listening/watching:
- ❑ unable to respond appropriately in improvisation/role play due to the need to process language before being able to process content
- ❑ lose track of what is spoken by whom in a studio or on screen
- ❑ unable to concentrate on listening/watching due to visual distractions and

background noise
- ❑ seem not to listen in discussion/brainstorming groups

Additional listening/watching issues:

Talking:

buts

- ❑ lose track of talk – often repeating themselves or 'drying up' completely
- ❑ struggle to use correct vocabulary –feel humiliated when words are mispronounced or the 'wrong' word is used
- ❑ difficulty with waiting for cues – interrupting others or speaking out of turn because lines may be forgotten when waiting
- ❑ fail to join in discussions as a planned comment is no longer relevant

Additional talking issues:

BARRIERS TO LEARNING - STUDY SKILLS ISSUES

Processing:

- ❑ take longer than others to respond to direction/instructions
- ❑ difficulty planning, sequencing and keeping to a story line when improvising/ developing coherent scripts
- ❑ misinterpret written instructions – leading to e.g. carrying out the wrong task
- ❑ tire more quickly than others when reading/writing so that the quality of work deteriorates over the course of a lesson
- ❑ sacrifice originality and creativity to complete an activity in the time allowed

Additional processing issues:

Working memory:

- ❑ poor working memory, so unable to remember lines and direction/instructions from one moment to the next
- ❑ forget what character to represent
- ❑ difficulty remembering to carry props etc. on to the stage
- ❑ misunderstanding complex sequences of instructions
- ❑ struggle to carry out a sequence of actions in the right order

Additional memory issues:

BARRIERS TO LEARNING - PRACTICAL ACTIVITIES ISSUES

Organisational:

- ❑ difficulty organising work space – misplace props and equipment
- ❑ difficulty finding/keeping the place in a script, locating director's notes in a workbook or finding files on a computer
- ❑ unable to cope with stage directions – e.g. left/right, forward/back etc. – so may be unable to move as directed or direct others effectively
- ❑ difficulty following a sequence of instructions in the right order, with an adverse impact on stage movement and directing skills
- ❑ sacrifice originality and creativity to complete an activity in the time allowed

Additional organisation issues:

Motor Skills:

- ❑ clumsy, bump into things or knock them over on stage or in a studio space
- ❑ unable to co-ordinate movements or plan sequential movements when using props/equipment
- ❑ experience problems with automaticity of fine and gross motor skills resulting in clumsiness when using e.g. cameras or a lighting desk
- ❑ experience weaknesses and increasing fatigue with some aspects of stage movement

Additional motor skills issues: